ONE BIG
ADVENTURE

Written by
CARISSA POTTER

Illustrated by
SASH AMEERCHUND

TO WYATT, DAKOTA, AND TUCKER.
GRATEFUL THAT MY PART IN HIS
STORY INCLUDED YOU.
— C.P.

DO YOU EVER DREAM ABOUT BEING A CHARACTER IN YOUR FAVORITE STORY?

I do. I imagine what it would be like to be a brave king on a noble quest or a sailor searching for hidden treasure deep in the sea.

RIES

MY FAVORITE STORY OF ALL IS GOD'S STORY.

It is full of many short stories that fit together to form one BIG story! God's story is true. It began before the earth was formed and is still being written today. In God's story, He uses followers of Jesus to share His love with people from every nation, tribe, and language.

I don't have to dream about being a character in God's story. I already am!

YOU CAN BE, TOO.

Let me introduce you to some of my friends around the world who have important roles in God's story.

SOFIA

VICTOR

ARIANNA

SUNG MIN

AMIRA

Hi, I am **SOFIA!** My family
and I live in Germany.

One day, while playing
at the park, we met
a family from Syria. They
had to flee from war to find
safety here in Germany.

My parents invite them over for
dinner every month. While our
parents talk, I show Aaliyah how
to play my favorite games and she
teaches me new words in Arabic.
Aaliyah's family has never learned
about Jesus, so my dad invited them to
study the Bible with us.

SOFIA

AALIYAH

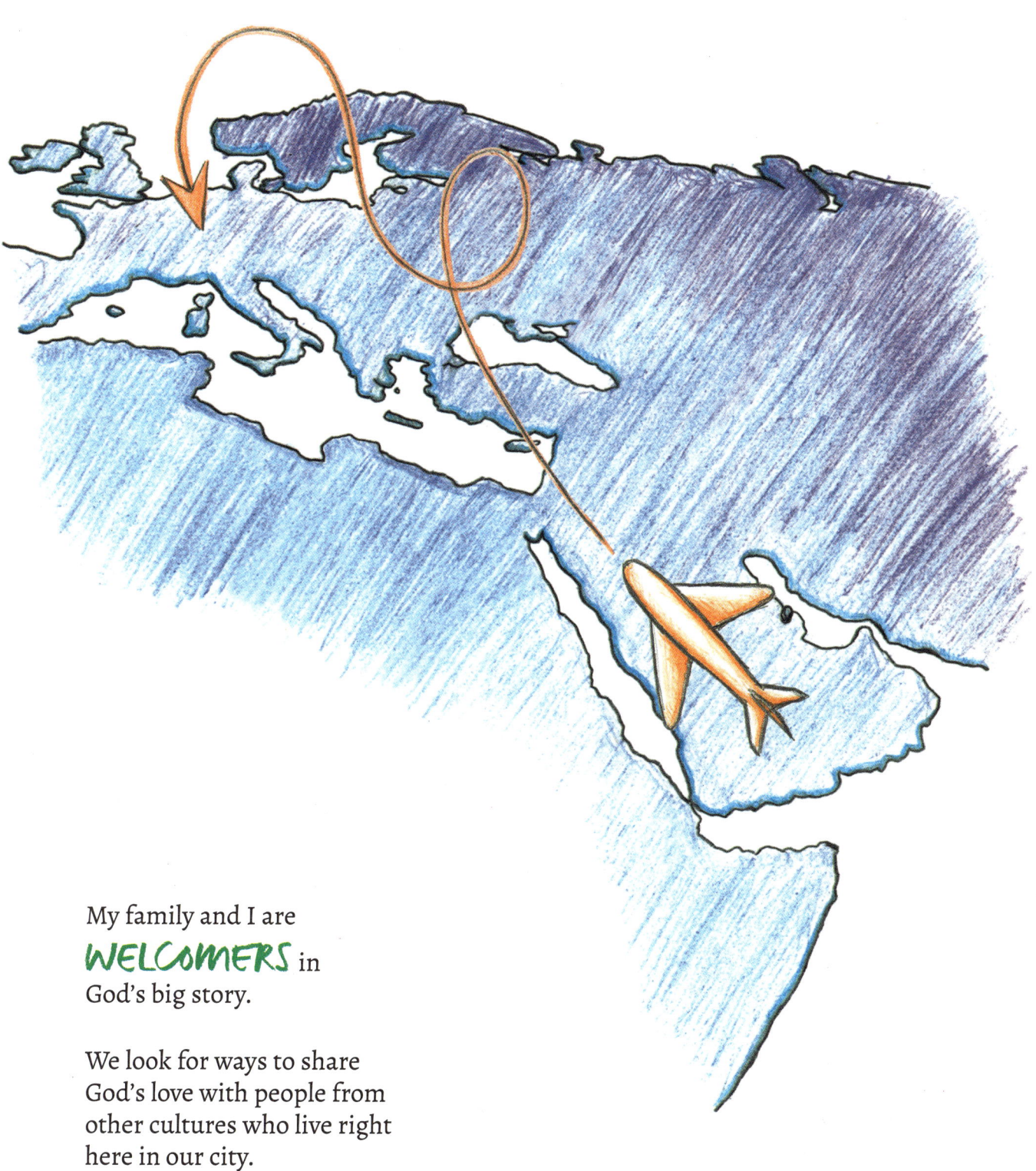

My family and I are **WELCOMERS** in God's big story.

We look for ways to share God's love with people from other cultures who live right here in our city.

My name is **SUNG MIN.** My family lives in South Korea.

Every month, we learn about a new people group — where they live, what they believe about God, and what life is like for them.

This month, we are learning about the Ansari people. Mom made us spicy lentil stew, an Ansari favorite. Dad is helping me make a kite to fly just like the Ansari children do.

After dinner, my family gathers around our world map and prays that Ansari families will have the chance to learn about Jesus, the God who loves them.

SUNG MIN

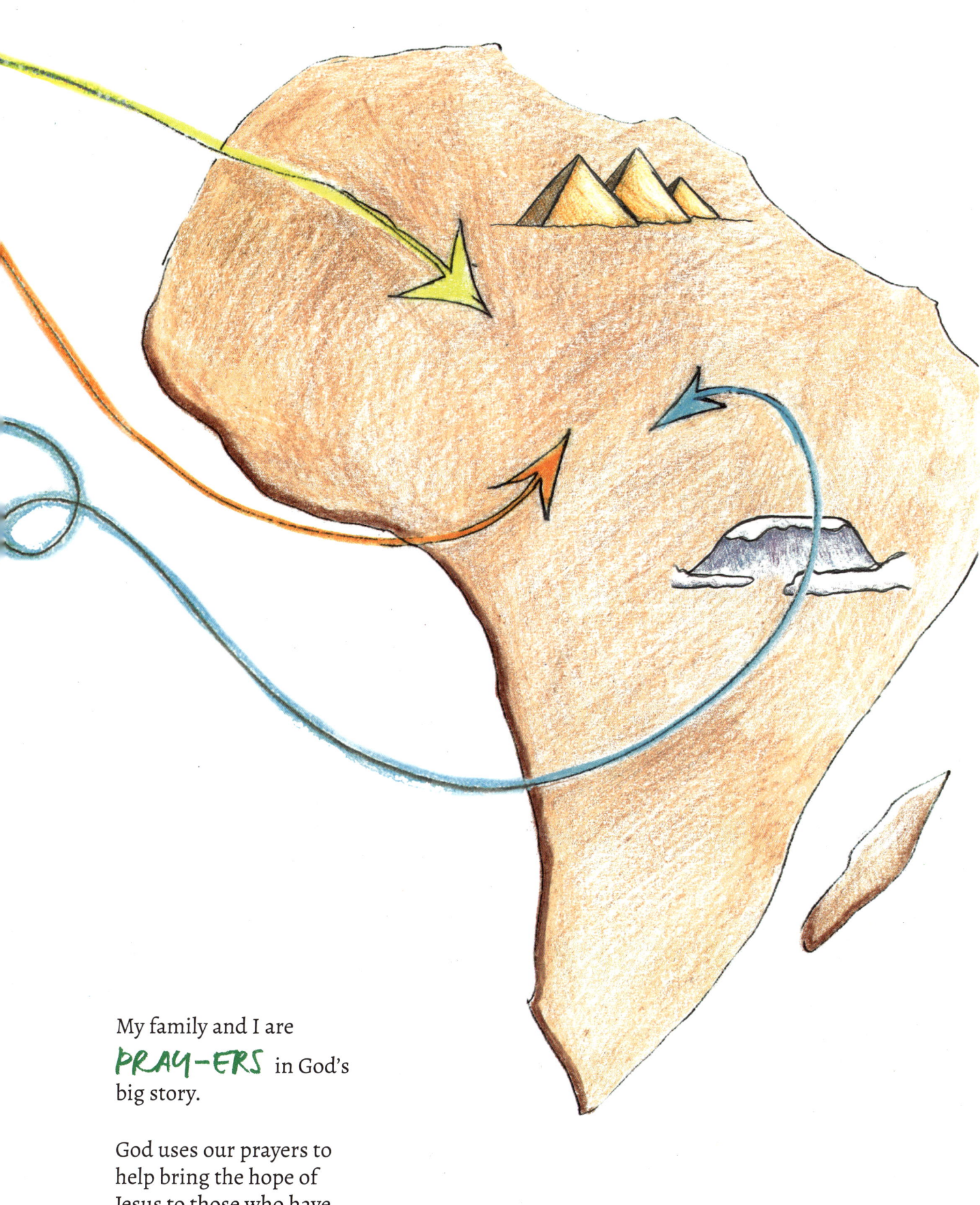

My family and I are **PRAY-ERS** in God's big story.

God uses our prayers to help bring the hope of Jesus to those who have not yet heard.

ARIANNA

Hi, I am **ARIANNA.** My family lives in Peru.

When I was little, my family and I learned about a people group in the Middle East who had no Bibles or churches where they could learn about Jesus in their own language.

We prayed that God would send followers of Jesus to help start a church there. The more we prayed, the more we knew that the family God wanted to send was us!

This year, we've been learning to speak the language of this people group. Soon, our family will leave Peru and move to the other side of the world to live among them and tell them about the God who loves them.

My family and I are GOERS
in God's big story.

We are leaving our home to go
and live among people who
have not had the chance to
learn about Jesus.

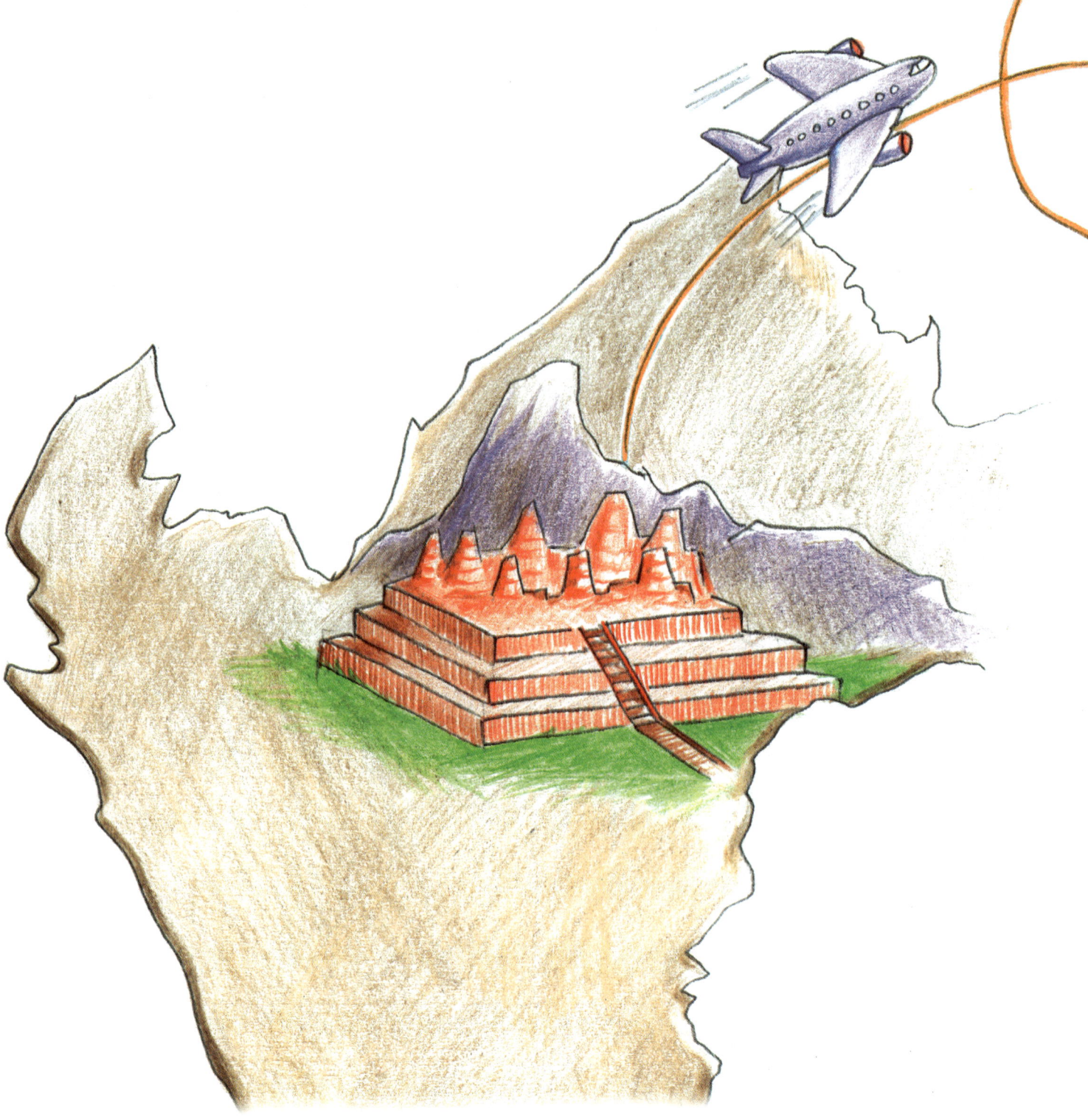

My name is **VICTOR.** My family and I live in Nigeria.

We know a woman from our church who moved to Indonesia as a goer. She is sharing about God's love with a people group who does not know about Jesus.

VICTOR

My family understands that she is doing important work, so we pray for her and give money every month toward her ministry.

Now she is working with a team to translate the Bible into the people's language so they can read God's Word for themselves. My sister and I asked our neighbors if we could water their plants to earn extra money for the translation project.

My family and I are **SENDERS** in God's big story.

We pray for goers and use our resources to meet their needs and fund projects that help people have the chance to learn about Jesus.

AMIRA & HER MOM

Hi, I am **AMIRA.** My family and I live in Pakistan.

Our family loves being a part of God's big story. We want to help other families learn how they can be a part of it too!

At church, I help Mom teach my class about what God is doing around the world. My father and big brother lead a Bible study with men and help them learn about God's story.

Every week, our family spends time praying for different unreached people groups. We always invite other families to come and pray with us.

AMIRA'S DAD & BROTHER

AMIRA TEACHES HER FRIENDS
TO PRAY FOR THE NATIONS

AMIRA'S MOM EXPLAINS GOD'S HEART
FOR THE WORLD IN THE BIBLE

My family and I are
MOBILIZERS
in God's big story.

We want every family in our church to know about God's love for all peoples and to find a role in God's story.

AMIRA'S DAD
SAYS GOODBYE
TO GOERS HE
ENCOURAGED TO
GO TO NEPAL

GOER

SENDER

DO YOU WANT TO BE A PART OF GOD'S BIG STORY, TOO?

No matter where you live or what your family looks like, there is a role for you.

God uses families just like yours to help others learn about Him. Being a part of God's story is one *big* adventure!

What a great day it will be when there are families from every people group who love Jesus!

DO YOU HEAR THAT?

God is inviting you and your family to be a part of His BIG story.

ALL YOU HAVE TO DO IS SAY YES!

A NOTE TO PARENTS

From Bible times to the present day, God has been at work fulfilling His mission to make Himself known among all nations. In every generation, God chooses to use families just like yours to accomplish His plans. This resource helps you and your children explore five different ways that families can be involved in God's mission: welcoming, praying, going, sending, and mobilizing. Collectively, these practices are called *World Christian habits.*

World because these practices are grounded in a biblical view of God's heart for the world and His global purposes, and flow from a desire to see God glorified among the nations.

Christian because these practices are for all believers, not just for pastors, seminary students, missionaries, or adults.

Habits because these are not one-time actions, but are ongoing practices that become part of everyday life.

By engaging with God in His work, we step into our chapter of His big story. When we as families introduce and establish these World Christian habits in our own homes, we get to be a part of fulfilling the Great Commission. In Matthew 28:19-20, Jesus says:

"Therefore go and make disciples of all nations, baptizing them in the name of the Father and of the Son and of the Holy Spirit, and teaching them to obey everything I have commanded you. And surely I am with you always, to the very end of the age."

This is not just Jesus' commission to the disciples, but also to us. Our families are called to be a part of bringing the gospel to all nations.

God is calling your family to live out your unique role in His story. He enables you by the power of His Holy Spirit, He promises to be with you until the end of the age, and He blesses your family with everything you need to live as World Christians. Take a closer look at each World Christian habit and explore how your family can develop them in your home and practice them in the world.

HOW TO USE THIS RESOURCE

1. After you read the storybook, use the following pages to reflect on the five World Christian habits as a family. Ask kids which habit is their favorite. Discuss why these practices are called habits and how habits are developed.

2. Pray together and ask God to show you how to incorporate these practices into your family life.

3. Use the verses and questions provided for each habit as a family devotion series. Discuss how each World Christian habit connects to completing the Great Commission.

4. Try some of the suggested activities with your family. Work together to think of your own ideas, and write them on the lines provided.

WELCOMING

Welcomers: People who take the time to get to know those from other cultures—students, professionals, refugees, and families—who are living in their country. Welcomers practice hospitality, meet needs, and look for opportunities to introduce their international friends to Jesus.

HOW DOES THIS HELP COMPLETE THE GREAT COMMISSION?

* Often we are living in the same city with people from other cultures and people groups who have never had access to the gospel.
* We take the time and effort to befriend them, demonstrate what it looks like to love and follow Jesus in everyday life, and share the gospel.

WHAT DOES THE BIBLE SAY ABOUT WELCOMING?

* **Leviticus 19:34, Deuteronomy 10:18-19** What do these verses reveal about God's heart for foreigners? Who are the foreigners living among us?
* **1 Kings 8:41-43** How does God feel about the prayers of foreigners? How can we see the foreigners in our midst as precious people created in the image of God?

HOW CAN OUR FAMILY PRACTICE WELCOMING?

* Befriend people who are from another country or culture.
* Invite someone from another culture to your home for dinner.
* Become a learner about other cultures and religions.

WHAT ELSE CAN WE DO AS A FAMILY?

_____

_____

_____

_____

_____

_____

_____

_____

GOING

Goers: People who labor to reach those of a culture significantly different from their own with the truth of Jesus. Most often, this involves traveling or moving to a distant area as a global worker.

HOW DOES THIS HELP COMPLETE THE GREAT COMMISSION?

* We go directly to the unreached and live among them to share the gospel.
* We disciple new believers and plant churches.

WHAT DOES THE BIBLE SAY ABOUT GOING?

* **Mark 16:15** What has God commissioned all believers to do?
* **Psalm 96:3-5** Where should we proclaim God's glory? Why should we proclaim it?
* **1 Peter 3:15** Why should we always be prepared to share our faith in Jesus? How can we prepare?

HOW CAN OUR FAMILY PRACTICE GOING?

* Take your family on a short-term trip.
* Pray a prayer of willingness to go.
* Find someone who is a goer and talk to them. Have them share their story with your family.
* Read child-friendly biographies of goers who went to unreached peoples.
* Learn to share your faith with others.

WHAT ELSE CAN WE DO AS A FAMILY?

_____

_____

_____

_____

_____

_____

_____

_____

_____

PRAYING

Pray-ers: People who consistently intercede for specific goers, for unreached people groups, and for more laborers to go and spread the gospel where it has never been heard.

HOW DOES THIS HELP COMPLETE THE GREAT COMMISSION?

* Our prayers work with God's purposes to accomplish His will.
* We use the gift of intercession to join God in directly affecting change in all the earth.
* We learn to listen to God and pray in agreement with His will. We become a vital part of bringing God's kingdom on earth.

WHAT DOES THE BIBLE SAY ABOUT PRAYING?

* **James 5:16-18** What happened when Elijah prayed? What does this say about prayer? What does this say about God?
* **Luke 10:2** What is the harvest this verse is talking about? Who are the workers? Why should we pray for workers to go into the harvest field? What are things we can pray for goers?
* **Matthew 6:9-10** How does this verse tell us to pray for our world?

HOW CAN OUR FAMILY PRACTICE PRAYING?

* Learn about specific unreached people groups so that you can pray for them.
* Incorporate regular intercessory prayer time.
* Pray for more laborers for the harvest (Luke 10:2).
* Gather around a world map to pray for unreached people groups.
* Use current events to inform your prayers for the unreached.

WHAT ELSE CAN WE DO AS A FAMILY?

_____

_____

_____

_____

_____

_____

_____

_____

© 2018 Weave. A ministry of the Center for Mission Mobilization. mobilization.org

SENDING

Senders: People who volunteer their resources to support the work of goers and the overall task of completing the Great Commission. Senders serve goers by praying for them and their work, giving money, and caring for their needs.

HOW DOES THIS HELP COMPLETE THE GREAT COMMISSION?

* We help fund and pray for those who are going.
* We help workers to focus on their mission and remain on the field long-term.
* We can give practical care and regular encouragement to keep goers healthy.

WHAT DOES THE BIBLE SAY ABOUT SENDING?

* **Romans 10:14-15** What two roles are involved in getting the gospel to someone?
* **3 John 5-8** What is the relationship between sender and goer?
* **2 Corinthians 9:7, 1 Chronicles 29:14** How should we give? Where do our possessions come from?
* **Colossians 4:3, 2 Thessalonians 3:1-2** How can we pray for the ministry of goers?

HOW CAN OUR FAMILY PRACTICE SENDING?

* Find a specific need of a goer and raise money to meet it.
* Get on the mailing list of a goer and pray regularly as a family.
* Develop a habit of setting aside money designated for God's work among the unreached.
* Support a goer on a monthly basis.

WHAT ELSE CAN WE DO AS A FAMILY?

_____

_____

_____

_____

_____

_____

_____

_____

_____

 **MOBILIZING**

Mobilizers: People who are passionate about God's global heart and purposes. They live in such a way to advance God's kingdom and help other believers to get personally connected to a role in completing the Great Commission.

HOW DOES THIS HELP COMPLETE THE GREAT COMMISSION?

* We cast vision for the part of the task that remains.
* We increase awareness of unreached peoples and their needs.
* We get more people involved in God's work in the world.

WHAT DOES THE BIBLE SAY ABOUT MOBILIZING?

* **1 Corinthians 12:27** Who can be involved in what God is doing in the world? Why should we all take part?
* **2 Timothy 2:2** What can we learn from the way Paul mobilized others?
* **1 Corinthians 11:1** Why should we ask others to follow or imitate us?
* **Revelation 7:9** If this verse is a promise of what is to come, how does this motivate us now?

HOW CAN OUR FAMILY PRACTICE MOBILIZING?

* Invite another family to join you in interceding for unreached peoples.
* Invite other families to join you in a project for a goer.
* Go through *Xplore* (Find at mobilization.org) with another family.
* Share the *Big Story Series* with another family.

WHAT ELSE CAN WE DO AS A FAMILY?

_____

_____

_____

_____

_____

_____

_____

_____

© 2018 Weave. A ministry of the Center for Mission Mobilization. mobilization.org

YOUR FAMILY HAS A PART TO PLAY IN GOD'S BIG STORY

Don't miss it. Live it out together
with *The Big Story Series.*

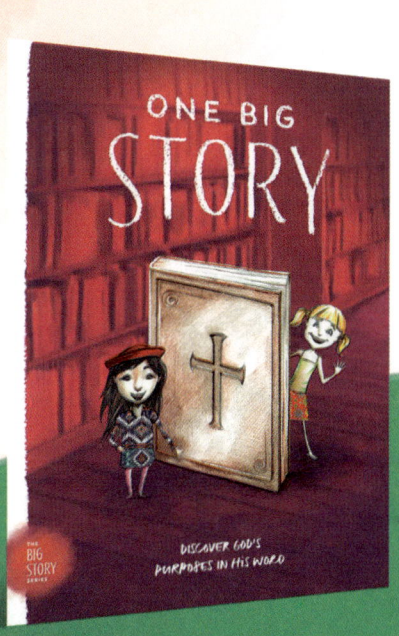

DISCOVER GOD'S
PURPOSE IN HIS WORD
THROUGH 52 BIBLE
STORIES THAT SHOW HIS
LOVE FOR ALL PEOPLES.

EMBRACE GOD'S LOVE FOR
THE WORLD THROUGH
INTERACTIVE LESSONS ON
WORLD RELIGIONS AND
UNREACHED PEOPLE GROUPS.

EXPLORE YOUR FAMILY'S
ROLE IN GOD'S STORY
AND LEARN TO LIVE IT
OUT IN EVERYDAY LIFE.

Purchase the entire Big Story Series or download for free at weavefamily.org/BigStorySeries

One Big Adventure: Explore Your Role in God's Work
from the *Big Story Series*

Copyright © 2018 Center for Mission Mobilization

Published by CMM Press
P.O. Box 3556
Fayettteville, AR 72702
cmmpress.org

Printed in the United States

First Edition, First Imprint, 2018

C: 05-08-18 M: 09-19-18 12:33 PM

One Big Adventure is a resource of the Center for Mission Mobilization. mobilization.org

Weave is a ministry of the CMM that exists to connect everyday families to the global story of God.

Weave would like to thank nine global partners who provided valuable feedback and cultural insight in the development of these resources and 14 families from seven different countries who field-tested selected activities in their homes.

We desire to make this material available to as many as will use it around the world in a way that honors everyone involved in the work. If you would like to translate or adapt this resource to use in your cultural context, we are very open to collaborating with you. There are guidelines for translators at mobilization.org/translation.

Please contact us at resources@mobilization.org.

ISBN: 978-1-947468-29-0

Printed in the United States of America.